CUBA

The Special Period

MARCIA FRIEDMAN

Published in the United States of America by
Samuel Book Publishers
Suite 125
630 S. Whitney Way
Madison, WI 53711

Editor: Larry Edgerton
Graphic Production: Hillary Friedman

Publisher's Cataloging in Publication

Friedman, Marcia L.
      Cuba : the special period / Marcia Friedman. -- 1st ed.
      photographs and text by Marcia Friedman
         p.   cm.
      ISBN 0-9657250-0-6
      1. Cuba--Pictorial works. 2. Cuban Americans--Personal narratives.
      I. Title
  .. F1765.3.F75 1998   917.291
                    QBI97-40453

Printed in Hong Kong

In memory of my father
Stanleigh Friedman zt"l

CONTENTS

PROLOGUE

With the collapse of the Soviet Union, billions of dollars of financial, economic, and military aid spent supporting Cuba came to a sudden halt. With no economic infrastructure to rely upon, the country was devastated. Dependent upon the millions of tons of Russian subsidized oil, Cuba's industry came to a standstill. Transportation reverted to the heavy usage of human and animal energy with bicycles and donkey-drawn carts traversing the streets; oxen displaced tractors in the fields; and production in all areas was greatly curtailed, if not entirely strangled. Staggering from the blow, Cuba hobbled along.

In October 1990, the commander-in-chief of the longest standing communist regime in the western hemisphere came forward and announced that the country had entered a "special period in time of peace." And Castro told the Cuban people they must make sacrifices and they must be patient. This crisis would pass, but until it did, the economy would operate as if in a state of war.

Up until this time, sacrifices had been made, restraint accepted, and difficult hardships endured for the false promise of a better tomorrow. Now in this gravely stricken economy, even greater sacrifices are made, more stringent restraints are implemented, and more severe hardships are borne, not for the sake of ideological guise, but for the simple struggle for daily subsistence.

Once one of the most developed of the Latin American countries during the pre-communist period when free enterprise flourished, life in Cuba under Castro's regime has plummeted into an abysmal third-world existence. And in this classless society, class distinctions exist: Castro's favored are allowed food, services, liberties, and goods denied to the tourists; tourists are allowed food, services, liberties, and goods denied to the Cubans; and the Cubans are denied.

Under tight control of the feared military regime, as the *Special Period* lingers on with little or no relief in sight, the Cuban people remain patient—a virtue not acquired, but commanded.

I visited Cuba at a time when the *Special Period* was no longer a temporary crises but a way of life. It has become a country where the outside world, though scrutinized, is allowed to come inside, but those inside can look out only through censured screens . . . wanting, hoping, and waiting. With my camera I tried to capture a place and people frozen in time: a people with the ability, education, and desire to propel themselves and their country into the prosperous technologically advanced country it could be. And while they wait, the world watches. Perhaps the exposures in this book will help reveal what the Cuban sees.

Marcia Friedman

INTRODUCTION

That night they gave us our orders and the battalion commander revealed the details of our covert voyage into history. The mood was tense as we learned the exact site of our landing—the Bay of Pigs. Even the bravest among us suppressed silent signs of hidden fear despite the overt display of excitement, pride, patriotism, and the strong belief that all that mattered was what we were about to do. And it was. The idealism of youth curdled in my veins. I was eighteen years old.

A few days earlier we had set forth aboard aged merchant marine vessels, from our staging area in Puerto Cabezas, Nicaragua. Cuba awaited only 550 nautical miles north by northeast. While lost in thought flitting between reflection and anticipation, we watched our convoy dauntlessly as it forged its way across the sea. The tranquility of the water was deceiving; it only calmed the obstinate night.

Just as we reached our destination, the furtive plan of landing under cover of darkness erupted into a fiasco. War planes showed up with the first rays of light and dove toward our defenseless vessels, strafing us with rockets and gunfire. Amid the shrieks and moans of the startled troops, our ship became a flaming inferno. Those who could jumped into the blazing waters and tried to swim ashore. Only the more fortunate made it.

Mass confusion reigned as we scattered for cover in the swamp where we had landed. Under the rain of shells, a few of us managed to avoid the random firing and reached a secluded area of the marshes. There we stood our ground until the ammunition ran out. Then the fighting mercifully halted, but not the struggle for survival.

With no food or fresh water, we scrambled deeper inland, trudging barefoot across scathing coral rocks and piercing thorns. The excruciating pain from the shredded skin on the bottom of my feet was masked only by the unmitigated thirst. Body fluids were our sole source of liquids, and we rang out our perspiration-soaked T-shirts for a few precious drops.

We endured in that muck for nearly three weeks, eating anything that crawled or twitched. The vegetation was inedible, and the lack of fresh water and nourishment eventually drove us out of the swamps toward more civilized land. But civilization came at a cost; our freedom was short lived. We were captured and sentenced to thirty years. And in my beloved Cuba, an old Spanish prison became my home.

When I left Cuba and came to the United States in 1960, it was with the impassioned intention of going back to liberate my country from communism. We did not succeed. I don't know how long I would have languished in that impregnable bastion if the U.S. Government hadn't ransomed us.

The 1961 Bay of Pigs Invasion is now but a memory. More than thirty-five years have passed, yet the images are still strikingly vivid. Though the fervor of my youth has waned, my commitment to Cuba is indelible.

I am a Cuban exile—a Cuban American—and have been now for most of my life. To the more than one million Cuban exiles living in America, there are few definitive answers to their nation's predicament. Beyond the consensus that as long as Castro remains in power there can be no hope for meaningful change, we indeed vary in our approaches to Cuba's present quandary. Some feel that by helping our fellow Cubans, we legitimize Castro's de facto regime and buttress his hold on power. Others feel that we exiles have a moral obligation to place humanitarian concerns above politics and should help our brothers and sisters in the island at this most difficult historical juncture.

Our diversity of opinion may not be unique, but the Cuban diaspora is. We share the uniqueness of our exile identity—a defining bond that, regardless of where we settled, we all share. We also share the ubiquitous love of our homeland. While our kindred spirit agonizes about the fate of those in the island, Cubans on both sides of the Florida Straits wonder when this nightmare will end. But for now, Cuba is a place of human despair and physical decay.

Marcia Friedman captures the essence of my country's present state of affairs and hints of her past glory through beautiful and poignant photography. This is Cuba—the *Special Period*. My heart goes out to her and to her people—my people.

Miguel Gonzales-Pando
Cuban Living History Project
Florida International University

$\mathcal{I}$t was a good time to be in Cuba—McDonald's wasn't there yet. It was a bad time to be in Cuba—McDonald's wasn't there yet. There are small and subtle signs of limited privatization, perhaps symbolic of a time to come, perhaps a pose. But for now, poverty is everywhere and ever present.

Life is difficult at best; dangerous at worst. One cannot speak too loudly or harshly or controversially about either the government or the trying situation. Nor can one be seen too much nor too long with foreigners; nor read, nor listen to, nor watch "propaganda" from the outside world during this relentless cycle of economic crisis euphemistically called the *Special Period*.

An address was written on a 3x5 piece of scratch paper, and the section of that paper where the writing occurred was meticulously torn off. The scrap of clean paper remaining could still be used and was put atop the small tablet. It was secured in place by a pebble gathered from the permanent rubble outside. Even a paper clip is rare.

Outside and inside, in every part of every city and every village, walls are crumbling, cracked, and in desperate need of paint. Houses once stately and grand now stand in neglect and disrepair. Cuba is a country of worn and torn-up roads and streets, empty stores, intermittent electricity, tattered and tarnished goods, and nothing new. But paint and repair and napkins and toss-away goods from Goodwill are on the bottom of the list of needs in this country. Food and medicine, the basics of life, are at a premium here. The rest is superfluous.

Against this backdrop of bareness, a modicum of extravagance does exist—for the tourists. There are tourist areas such as hotels, resorts, and beaches, which are nice and new and kept so, or old and kept up. The tourist trade is a hope for redemption, and the desire for foreign investment a double-edged necessity. But restrictions abound for tourist and Cuban alike. The tourist, however, can leave. The Cubans, in essence, cannot.

In Cuba there is no freedom of speech, no freedom of the press. There are restrictions on life and liberty, and it is a country where happiness, and not the pursuit thereof, is mandated. All creatures are hungry. Everything is rationed. Deprivation and deterioration are the state of affairs; and the comfort in which the tourists tread, the Cubans dare not go.

Silence is ubiquitous. The streets are quiet. The country is still. Truths are heard in surreptitious whispers while everyone waits, listening for the footsteps of change.

CUBA. The country of sun, sea, and song—how it used to be.

CUBA. The country of sun, sea, and song—it still is.

HAVANA

From far
and near
and long ago
and now
in disrepair,
yet what was once
still is somewhere
a pretty street
of flowered trees
and buildings with a flare,
not everywhere,
but colorful
and cars that barely go
of long ago, or so it seems,
and people wait for shops to open,
shops in short supply,
a butcher and a cow, perhaps, if not, another week goes by,
and bars,
is this the vision he had seen,
looking from without
within,
what bars can do, have done,
when barred
from wealth and freedom
emptiness survives,
yet beauty thrives in Cuba
and in the shadows songs are sung.

From far

and near

and long ago

and now

in disrepair,

yet what was once

still is somewhere

a pretty street

of flowered trees

and buildings with a flare,

not everywhere,

but colorful

and cars that barely go

of long ago, or so it seems,

and people wait for shops to open,

shops in short supply,

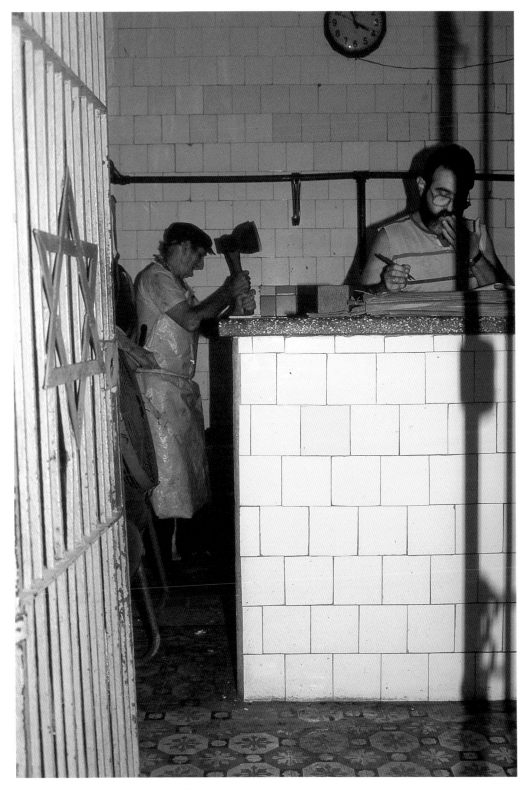

a butcher and a cow, perhaps, if not, another week goes by,

and bars,

is this the vision he had seen,

looking from without

within,

what bars can do, have done,

when barred

from wealth and freedom

emptiness survives,

yet beauty thrives in Cuba

and in the shadows songs are sung.

SANTIAGO de CUBA

Transportation
is anything that moves
or could
or would
or doesn't
or is crammed
upon a city thoroughfare,
a square where
waiting for the future
is a way of life
upon a quiet street
of inner strife,
where a home,
a house once grand,
once kempt,
once lived in
is now a school, now the government's
a place of show where tourists go
and privileged partying children have ice cream
while other children dream
about a glow
after the rain
when poverty is washed away
and light will flow through every window
on every city street,
and to the mountains and behind to find
a better life, not just a painting
in the imagination of one's mind,
for with faith from out the shadow seeps the brilliance of the light
as a fort
does not a prison make
and the music keeps on playing through the darkness of the night.

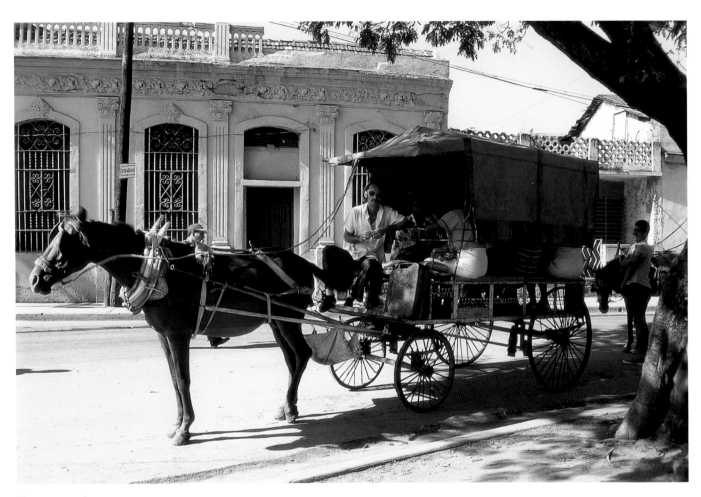

Transportation

is anything that moves

or could

or would

or doesn't

or is crammed

upon a city thoroughfare,

a square where

waiting for the future

is a way of life

upon a quiet street

of inner strife,

where a home,

a house once grand,

once kempt,

once lived in,

is now a school, now the government's

a place of show where tourists go

and privileged partying children have ice cream

while other children dream

about a glow

after the rain

when poverty is washed away

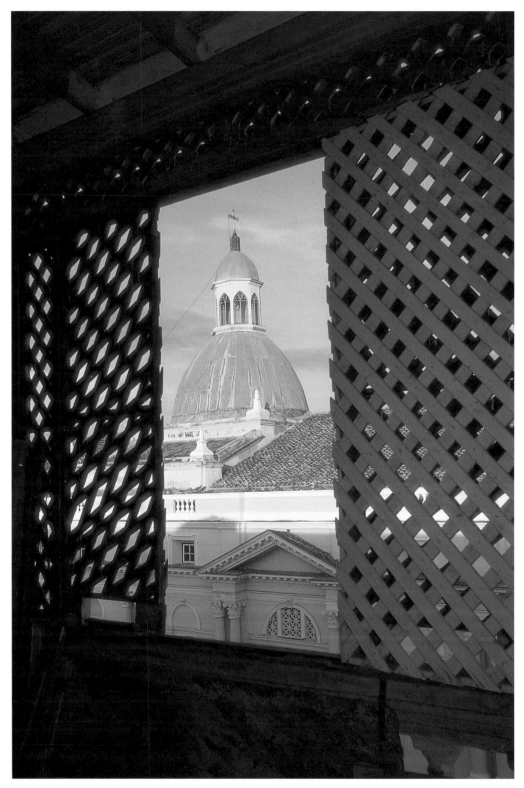

and light will flow through every window

on every city street,

and to the mountains and behind to find

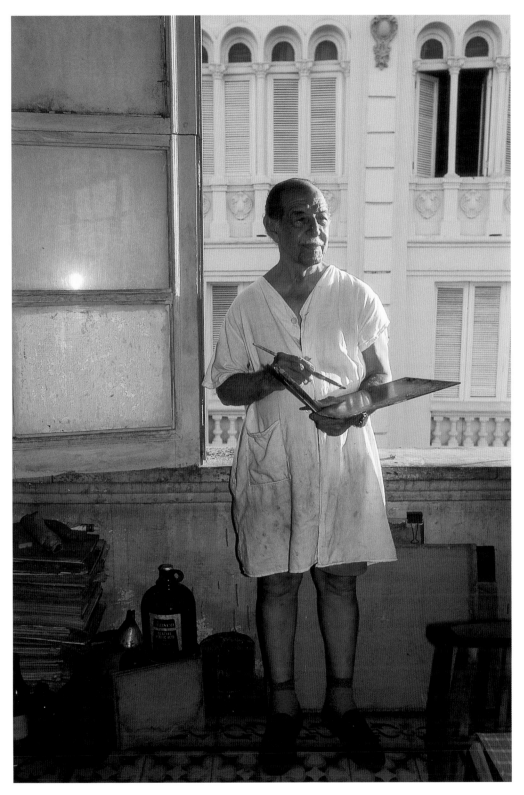

a better life, not just a painting

in the imagination of one's mind,

for with faith from out the shadow seeps the brilliance of the light

as a fort

does not a prison make

and the music keeps on playing through the darkness of the night.

VOICES from the EXILES

75

I came to the United States in 1960, when I realized Castro had betrayed the Revolution and established a communist regime. I did not think I would stay here more than a year, so I didn't bring anything with me. I had intended to return to Cuba. I still hope to spend my last days there living at the Hotel Nacional, near to where my old law office was.

I would like to return to Havana. In my younger days as editor-in-chief of *El Mundo* during the Batista years, there was much turmoil and upheaval. Castro's Revolution brought in an even tighter reign with more severe restrictions and controls. My prayer is to be able to return to the country of my birth and to live out my days in a Cuba of freedom and peace. Hopefully, that will come to pass.

Cuba was a rich country, and it has excellent soil and natural resources. If the people are hungry today, it is because Castro exports the national production in order to get hard currency. Cuba is exporting fish, lobster, and oranges, yet the Cubans themselves have none of these to eat. The little they have to eat allows them barely two meals a day, and the amount of rationed food is hardly sufficient for a meal. Even rice and beans are sparse commodities.

Cuba is not in its present terrible situation because of the U.S. embargo. The reason for the island's ruin has been Castro. Before he came to power, Cuba was one of the richest Latin American countries, and the most advanced. Conditions in Cuba are very bad, and the people are desperate because they have no future and no alternative. What's the use of studying to become doctors, engineers, or lawyers if at the peak of their career they can only make the equivalent of ten dollars a month? There are no incentives.

Castro used the resources he received from Russia to finance revolutions and to train terrorists in Latin America and Africa. He had armies in Angola and Ethiopia. He spent the money there instead of investing it in Cuba. During the thirty-five years when he was receiving huge subsidies from the Soviet Union, he never mentioned the embargo.

I agree with the embargo. The American people had investments in Cuba that the Castro regime confiscated. It's only natural that the U.S. does not want to do business with a crook. But the embargo doesn't prevent Castro from buying anything he wants. In fact, he can buy American products elsewhere, such as in Panama and Mexico. The real problem is that Cuba has no money and no credit. The embargo has not been the cause, nor is the United States responsible for that.

His regime has been a disaster. But in two areas Castro has been very successful. One is that he has created the most effective repressive system ever known. The regime controls every aspect of life from what the people must eat to where they must work. And, of course, the government has groups of vigilantes keeping constant watch over everything that goes on in their neighborhoods.

The other area in which Castro has been very effective is in creating a propaganda and public relations campaign capable of reaching every corner of the world. The problem is that he says one thing and does another. Actually, that was the way he seized power—by fooling everybody. In that respect he has been able to accomplish what seemed impossible: to fool all the people all of the time. Perhaps, in this too, he will fail.

Luis Botifoll

Iwas born in Cuba in 1932 and I left in 1960. Once they confiscated all of our property there, especially our plant, our equipment, our company, BACARDI, the whole family decided to leave. When I went to ask for the required exit permit, they not only denied me the permit, but they took my passport away and wouldn't allow me to leave. While I worked for BACARDI, I was a professor of chemical engineering at the University of Oriente, and it was a time when they were trying to prevent anyone who could contribute to the Revolution from leaving the island.

It was a very difficult time. I tried to persuade my wife to go ahead without me, but she did not want to leave me behind. I told her it would be easier to leave by whatever means I could, if I left alone, and that if we were to go together, it would be much more dangerous. I told her to go and I would meet her there. So my wife, my son, and my grandparents flew to Miami.

Eventually I left—illegally according to the laws of the Revolution—in a boat with five other people. It took us six days to get to the coast of Florida. My parents remained behind with my brother, whose wife had just had a baby. They had problems getting a U.S. visa because of the newly born baby, so they had to stay for a while. Finally they left.

On my mother's side, my great-great grandfather, Facundo Bacardi, came to Cuba in 1834. In 1862 the Bacardis established their first tiny distillery in Cuba, which continued operating until Castro's regime. By that time we had three distilleries in Cuba and had, fortunately, established distilleries in Puerto Rico and Mexico. So when our business in Cuba was confiscated, we continued to produce BACARDI rum elsewhere, but not the beer.

The plants are still there in Cuba and still operate as well as anything operates in Cuba under Castro's regime—they operate when and if they get hops, or malt, or molasses, or whatever. I guess what they sell domestically is without a label and unbranded, but they sell our beer in the dollar area using our trademark, HATUEY. There is nothing we can do about it.

I think that Castro is under tremendous pressure, and so he is making little concessions. I say little concessions because, for instance, out of ten foreign media applicants to operate inside Cuba for external transmission, he allowed one—CNN. So it was a gesture on his part to say, "You see, we've allowed one of you to operate here now." Are things changing? Not really. I would say that things will start to change if he allows that station to transmit into Cuba and let the Cuban people hear what the world has to say.

The importance of his allowing one foreign media representative to operate from Cuba is relative, and he knows very well it will not affect the Cuban people nor himself. This opening is only a little gesture. But the tides are turning against him; world opinion has changed, and he needs to regain some support. With these little concessions, he can make it appear as though he is changing.

It's very difficult to know what is inside his head, but outwardly he projects the confidence that socialism and communism will triumph. But that is so out of touch with reality, it is questionable whether he really believes it. Or whether he is just saying that, while deep inside he is simply trying to gain time to stay in power for as long as he can. Like Hitler when the Russians and Americans were bombarding Berlin, he was still commanding his officers in his bunker and saying, "The tide will turn and we'll win the war." Castro is a strong leader like Hitler was, but these are evil leaders, and they never give up.

He has these block committees, led by the security arm of the government, that control every block. Any new car that comes into that block is suspect and is reported. If there's a car that was never seen there before: Who does it belong to? Who is he? They investigate. The amount of money and effort the government devotes to such control and for security is enormous and is one of the reasons the country is failing. A vast amount of money is going to nonproductive activities just to keep the population under control.

People cannot speak against him or the regime, or they'll lose their jobs and go to jail. So there is no strongly organized opposition from within. Except for the government and the army, the only organization that has remained organized in Cuba is the Catholic Church. The Catholic Church was subdued and pushed into submission; the churches were closed, but the Church remained. Now the Church is beginning to speak.

For many, many years the Church did not speak. Many Cubans here resent the fact that the Catholic Church kept quiet. They felt it was the only way to survive, and so no one spoke out. Some priests are beginning to now, perhaps realizing that things are coming to an end, or at least closer to an end. A new cardinal has been appointed, the churches are reopening, and the Pope is going to visit Cuba in February.

To gain time, Castro needs to have these little pockets of support that he has lost, so it will seem that he is changing. All he wants is to have people say, "Don't rush him, he's changing," again, just to gain time. What Castro wants to do is to die in power. He doesn't care what happens after he dies. He's in his early 70s, and he wants to have another three years and maybe then another three, and so on. He's gambling for time, biding for time. He hopes that by the Pope's visit, the Catholic Church will not become a militant anti-Castro organization. Nothing will happen between now and the time the Pope comes in February because he needs the Pope, and both sides want the Pope to come. Castro has another year in his pocket.

The Catholic Church is not really opposition. There are some priests who have become light opposition, but the institution of the Church in Cuba is not openly opposing Castro's policies. However, the fact remains that it is well organized. People go to church every Sunday, and there are thousands and thousands of people who listen to what the priests say. And what they say could be the answer to our prayers.

Manuel Cutillas
Chairman, Bacardi Limited

My feeling is one of great love and great sadness. We have been living in this country for well over thirty years, and even though many of those years were hardship years, they were always good because from the day we came, we have always had reason to hope that tomorrow would be better than today. Everyone has been able to come here with that hope, and that hope drives people and creates happiness.

I feel great sadness about my brothers and sisters in Cuba today. There's no tomorrow that they can look to, to be better than today or yesterday. They live in a constant state of despair, and that makes us very sad and in many ways creates for us a deep psychological wound. Here we are enjoying so many things, from our freedom to basic foodstuffs, decent housing, and other things; and yet we know that our relatives, our friends, the people in Cuba are suffering hardship and deprivation.

Another part of the problem is the helplessness that we feel being here in exile. It is painful to see how much indifference there is to our plight from an international perspective. One would expect sympathy, especially from our brethren in Latin America who should be the first to rally to the cry of the people of Cuba for basic human rights and freedom, and for their right to choose—to simply choose who should be governing them.

I would like to see significant international pressure brought on Cuba to say to Fidel Castro, "Enough is enough." No human being has the right to govern a country for thirty-six years without the consent of the governed. "Step aside, hold free elections, allow the Cubans to choose." This is not a question of whether communism is good or bad; it's not a question of economics. It's a question of basic decency: the Cuban people should have what anyone else has—the right to choose their government. If Castro is elected in a free government, I'll be the first to support that, as much as I dislike him and his policies. But no one has the right to say, "I am President for life simply because I want to be," and to support that claim through sheer terror and a police state.

There has been so much misinformation about the embargo. We know the economic situation in Cuba is not the result of the embargo; it is the result of an economic system that is a total failure. For years Cuba has been able to buy anything it wants from any other country except the United States. Yet it has lacked the foreign reserves and the economic means to buy anything. A failure of the economic system in Cuba is not a result of the embargo; it is a result of the deficiencies of its own system. The embargo has served as a scapegoat.

Yet an embargo worked in South Africa, and it has worked in other places. It must be given time to work. For so many years Cuba was dependent upon the Soviet Union, who gave the Castro regime a constant artificial infusion of cash. It is only since the dissolution of the Soviet Union and the elimination of that artificial aid to the Cuban economy that the embargo has had time to have an effect. We have seen the cracks that it has opened and the potential that it is beginning to create. We need to make sure that we do not put Castro's system on artificial life support. It will die of its own accord.

What is extremely important is that the international community come together, not so much in the form of an embargo, but with an absolute resolve not to offer economic help to a country that doesn't deserve it. Let Castro buy anything he wants from anywhere, but let's not go to Cuba and give him all kinds of credits and give him all kinds of financial extensions on a system that doesn't work. It's the same thing as a business. If you see that a business is going down the tubes or is on the verge of bankruptcy and you know that it is totally mismanaged, would you come to the aid of that business? Would you give it a loan? Would you give it financial assistance? The answer is clearly no, because it is throwing good money after bad, and all you are doing is extending the plight of the people for five or ten more years, or even three.

What we need to do here in exile is to continue to show solidarity with our brothers and sisters in Cuba; to let them know that we care, that we love them, that we would like for them to enjoy the same opportunities that we are enjoying here. And that is the message. It's not a combative message, it's not an ideological message, it's a message of love; it's a message of fellowship with our people there that goes beyond politics and the government.

Carlos Salidrigas
CEO, Vincam Group, Inc.

The *Special Period* will last in Cuba until Castro defines it as another period. I don't see conditions there improving significantly in the near future. The Cubans themselves anticipate difficult years. Things may even get worse, or not improve at all.

Castro has always implemented the ration card in Cuba, but since the *Special Period,* there has been a dramatic change. Even though limited then, the things one could get with a ration card before are now not available at all. Quantities have been reduced significantly. Transportation has been affected, as have medical services; goods and services have been greatly affected.

For instance, doctors. You have many doctors now who are leaving the profession to work as clerks in the hotels or in the service industry. Some do it because they need the basics of life. But others leave due to frustration, because they don't have the means to practice their profession. Many of those working in the hospital don't even have bandages. When people in Cuba go to most hospitals, they are required to bring their own bed sheets, their own towels. Before Castro, it was one of the best systems in Latin America.

In my mind, the biggest problem Cuba has, besides the lack of freedom and human rights, is in the area of productivity. You can invest money in different ways, but until the country improves its productivity, you're throwing money away. That, coupled with large expenditures for things such as internal security forces, the army, foreign involvement with terrorists, rather than for food and the basic internal needs of the country, means that I don't see any change in the foreseeable future.

Obviously, the disappearance of Castro from power would be the beginning of the recovery of the country, economically, politically, and socially. But defeat is not an accepted concept in Castro's mind. Castro is firmly convinced that he is Cuba, and that it's inconceivable to think about Cuba, present or future, without his participation in it. It's inseparable for him. To him, he is Cuba and Cuba is Castro.

Guarioné M. Diaz
President/Executive Director
Cuban American National Council

We were inside the Cathedral. There was a large crowd of people inside at that mass to protest to what was happening. When we came out, the militia were there. They kicked and spit on us as they pushed us into the school. Once they managed to corral and get us inside, they locked us in and would not let us out. We were Catholics and they were against what we were preaching.

My father came and got me out. But that night they kept calling the house and telling me they were going to burn me and threatening to do other terrifying things to me. I was only 15. I could hear the sputtering of machine guns every night from my home as they killed people. One night one of our drivers was picked up by Castro's men four times. The next day his black hair had turned completely white. He died soon enough.

My father declared himself a counter-revolutionary and we had to leave. My sister came to the States first, then I came, and finally a year later we were able to bring my father. My cousin is Vilma Espin. She was the female communist leader who married Fidel's brother Raúl. She did not forewarn my father to leave Cuba, but we knew what she stood for and what was going on.

I was in a rare position: to be in Santiago and to be against Castro when Castro was in the mountains. We knew what Castro was and we were not in the mood that the country was. When Fidel came in, we were against him. I remember going to school one day and one of the nuns was expressing her happiness. I said to her, "Don't be, because you're going to leave this country before I do." And I saw it happen.

At lunch time I'd come home from school, and my father always had on the short wave radio. Che Guevara had a program during which he would delineate the points of the Revolution. If you were to look at these points, they were all communist dogma. But the people were blind to it. They were so emotionally involved in the fervor that they did not analyze what was actually taking place. If people really had listened to what was happening in Cuba, they would not have supported Castro. But they were more focused on getting Batista out than on what was taking place.

We have patients who come here for treatment from Cuba. They say they do not know how they can even be there, but they keep hoping that something is going to change. The other day I was talking to a priest who was telling me that he doesn't know what to do. Things are tightening up. Apparently there were ways to send medicines and get them directly to the people, but it is now more difficult to do. They cannot even get in basic needs. He has seen an increase in sickness and many more cases of malnutrition. These things cannot even be talked about. Everything must remain quiet and unspoken.

He said he is also witnessing a renaissance of faith in the people and more are coming to church. Even though they have never been exposed to Christianity, they are anxious and desirous of listening. People are looking for hope and for something that makes them go on. I spoke to a doctor who recently returned from a conference in Cuba, and the people pleaded with him, "Please do not forget us."

I don't think that we can do much today. I think that the only way Cuba is going to change is for the country to reach a point where it cannot tolerate the system anymore. But Castro has opened up religion; he has hooked up with markets outside of the United States—Canada, Spain—and is bringing in money, so I don't think it's going to happen very soon. Even though the country has gone through so much, and those people are in such misery, he is still strong. Unless he dies . . .

He is strong with the people, and they still follow him. I don't know what it is, but the man has charisma. That hasn't changed, but I don't know why they don't see him for what he is. Perhaps he's their only hope. Perhaps it's because that's the only world they know.

Just this past weekend I heard the situation was getting worse. I would love to help the people. It's a very emotional situation because you don't want to help the government, but the people really need it. Do we abandon them? It's very touchy. It's a difficult question. But if I can help, I will.

After Castro, I will go and visit. I will go back and help, but I do not think I will move back; I've made my life here. I don't think I'm ready to go back and start all over again. But I will definitely do whatever I have to in order to help people get on their feet. I don't think it's fair for me and others who left the country to go back and ask the people there to move out. I could not do that. There are many people thinking of going back and getting back what they lost. But that was our choice. We left. We should have stayed there if we really wanted those things. We wanted others to fight our fight. There were people who stayed because they agreed with the government, and others who could not leave, and others who would not and did not leave. We left.

Carolina Calderin
CEO, Pan American Hospital

The de Céspedes have been in Cuba a long time. I'm a fifth-generation descendant of Carlos Manuel de Céspedes, the President of Cuba who freed the slaves and brought war against Spain in the fight for independence. He is considered the father of the country.

I left Cuba as an 11-year-old child. In 1961 I was brought here along with 13,000 other children sponsored by the Catholic Church in a program called Pedro Pan. My parents were left behind. They were not allowed to leave because they were professionals. They didn't know if they would ever see us again. It was hard on us, but harder on the parents. We were just kids. Kids adjust.

I would love to go to Cuba, but I am heavily involved in anti-Castro movements. I am a director of the Cuban American National Foundation, which is an organization that disseminates truthful information about what's going on in Cuba. For years Castro had a field day broadcasting his own propaganda, but we've managed to turn the tide and show the world that the country is a disaster. I don't think I would be very welcome there.

In 1959 Cuba was a strong economic contender in the western hemisphere. He has set the country back to where it is now below Haiti as an economic power. For over thirty years, Russia gave Fidel Castro more than six billion dollars in aid. What does he have to show for it? Nothing! The road system is a fiasco; the airports are a fiasco; the telephone system is a fiasco; electricity is a fiasco; the water system is a fiasco. Nothing. He has nothing to show for it.

The number one priority confronting every Cuban when he wakes up in the morning is, "What are we going to eat today?" And the husband runs in this direction looking for a potato, and the wife runs in that direction looking for an egg. He keeps people busy and hungry and demoralized, so they don't have the wherewithal or the mental power to band together to do something about the situation. He's been very astute and conniving in accomplishing this. Being at the center of everything, he divides and conquers—constantly. He has totally destroyed, totally demoralized the people. They are defeated. He cannot love the Cuban people like he says he does; he cannot care about them.

The man is a proverbial liar. There is a video tape of forty-six men being shot to death by a firing squad, and we know he has killed thousands upon thousands more. Yet during an American television interview he did a few years ago, he denied it. When told of this tape, he finally admitted one or two people had been killed somewhere in the provinces. If a lie detector had been put on him at that moment, he'd probably have passed it because he believes his own lies. This man is not worth another chance. He has proven over the last thirty-six years that nothing, nobody is going to change him.

The embargo is not against the Cuban people; it is against the government. A good example is the recent hurricane. Cubans in Miami collected more than 240,000 pounds of foodstuffs in less than a week. He has allowed 70,000 pounds into the country. The items are still sitting here in a Miami warehouse. Now they're starting to send them to Santo Domingo because he will not allow them in. What man in his right mind would say "no" with hungry children to feed?

The Foundation has made a standing offer: we will ship $10 million worth of medicines and food to Cuba provided that he lets the Catholic Church or the Foundation distribute it. That offer was made years ago. He has never taken us up on it.

There are trained doctors in Cuba, but there's no medicine, and they have nothing there to operate with. Every day people come into our offices here who are going to Cuba to see a relative needing an operation. Theses relatives are told by their doctor, "You need this operation but you have to bring six syringes, three vials of antibiotics, a scalpel, and a box of sutures, or else I can't operate. There's nothing here to operate on you with."

He has thousands of political prisoners in jail. To get thirty years over there, you don't have to try very hard. Anyone who does the slightest thing—write something on the wall, a slogan against Castro—and he's got thirty years.

I think Castro's days are numbered. I don't know how it's going to happen, but I have a feeling that there is just so much that the people of that country can withstand.

Carlos M. de Céspedes
Chairman & CEO, Pharmed Group

Here we're Cuban-Americans. I consider myself a dual citizen. Obviously my first responsibility and my first loyalty are to the United States. It's my citizenship, it's my passport, it's where I live, it's where I pay taxes, it's where I have a social responsibility. That is a very logical, intellectual, and emotional tie.

I have another tie that works on deeper level, which is my responsibility to those and that which I left behind. And that is a continual dichotomy with which I struggle. To what degree can I take responsibility for what's happening there and help the people without helping the government or the regime perpetuate itself? I have two older aunts there, one in her late 80s and the other 92, and I know of their hunger. That's something I could help ameliorate with U.S. dollars. The fact that these U.S. dollars are going indirectly to the economy and to the regime is at war with the fact that these people need help. It is agonizing trying to reach a decision. But the human side has won.

I sent them U.S. dollars. They did not have the resources to buy the kind of food and medications that they need. I made a personal choice. All of us exiles are in this quandary of the swinging pendulum where one day we see one perspective, and the next, the other. Would I travel and spend money there? No.

In the broader sense, we have a responsibility to rebuild the country when the government changes. Some Cubans fear the exiles will return and reclaim their homes and properties. But distinctions can be made between personal and business property. There has to be a middle ground, a compromise on both sides. Unreasonable people are going to be unreasonable, but certainly reasonable people can come to an agreement. Between those of us who are here and those who are there, no group is going to get 100 percent of what they want. We're going to have to accept that going in. The question is whether we want to reunify Cuba more than we want a personal victory.

I came here on December 17, 1960, with my father, my mother, and my younger sister. I was nine years old. Cuba looked like Miami Beach to me when I left. I'm sure from a nine-year-old's perspective everything looked so much bigger, but nonetheless it certainly had not deteriorated as it has now. I look at these pictures and see a grand old lady who has aged miserably because she hasn't had access to technology and cosmetics and all the other benefits that most of the rest of the western world has access to, whereas at one time she had it all. So it is very sad. But I have hope for her; I have hope for her . . .

Ana Marie Fernandez Haar
CEO, IAC Advertising Group

I left Cuba on July 1, 1960. I went back for the first time in October 1996. I was invited by the bishop's conference to give a paper on the subject of the Catholic Church and Cuban nationality.

I was told by some priests in Cuba that there is now less discrimination against the Church. Perhaps Castro is using the church for political purposes to try to improve his public image. When the doors are being closed to him almost everywhere else in the world, this door still seems to be open. It is the one way he has to give the impression that he is not as repressive as the outside world claims.

Castro's followers first became disillusioned when they realized that what they were told during the golden days of socialism was false, and that the wealth of their nation did not come from their government, but from the Soviet Union. Hearing broadcasts from Miami radio stations about the world outside of Cuba strengthened that disillusionment with the government and the system. Yet many fear change.

People are frightened of what will happen in Cuba if there is drastic change. They fear anarchy. What they have there is stability. They have had almost forty years of stability. Peace. It might be peace like you have in the graveyards, but it is peace. People are afraid.

Bear in mind that there are hundreds of thousands of people whose lives depend on the government. If there is a drastic change, what are they going to do? Where are they going to go? What's going to become of them? Despite what people say, those people support the government. They have a stake in it. Then there is the fear held by many that returning exiles will take their homes from them. It is a very complex situation.

I think the only changes that will take place in Cuba are those that will be brought about by chronology. With the passage of time, there will be solutions to problems. But whatever transition takes place now or in the future should be a peaceful one, because the people have suffered enough.

José Hernandez
Professor Emeritus
Georgetown University

I was from Spain. As a boy, I joined the Jesuits. Prior to becoming ordained, we had to spend three years teaching as a way of knowing that you have the qualities to teach. It was for that I was sent to Cuba.

I arrived in Havana in 1942, the very same year that Fidel Castro came to Havana to begin studying at the Jesuit school, Colegio de Belén. He had started his studies in another Jesuit school in Santiago de Cuba, but came here for his last three years of high school. He was sixteen.

It was a boarding school, and I was given the position of having to take care of the boys. I also taught. I was not yet a priest. Even so, many people say, "Father Llorente was the spiritual leader of Fidel Castro." Well, not exactly. I was his spiritual advisor, his friend, and his teacher.

When we met, immediately we became very good friends. I saw in him that he was a very special boy . . . special . . . very special. He was idealistic and very ambitious to become the best in the school at whatever it was. For instance, he came from a school in Santiago where they only played soccer. In Havana they played more sports—basketball, baseball, track—as in the American schools. So he became immediately very interested in becoming a member of every team. He was very competitive, but in that moment, in a good way, not in a bad way.

He said to me, "Father, give me extra time. Father, is it possible that when they go to bed, I can stay and practice basketball? Could you put a light in the court for me?" "Of course, yes." I always pushed him to become better in the things he liked. He needed that. I was in that moment innocent, so to speak. I thought that all those things he was interested in becoming were very important and very good. So I helped him to be the best in any way I could.

He started practicing basketball, then track, then baseball, and he became a member of the different teams, and one of the best, though without special style. He is not sophisticated in such things, but he wins. It's part of his personality. For instance, the best five in basketball played very nicely, and the coach always liked to start the game with these five. But Fidel was sitting down there too. And when problems came, the coach would say, "Fidel, come out." And he would go.

One day it was the final game between two finalist high school teams from all of Cuba, and the game was celebrated in the new Sport Palace on the Malecón. The other team was a Protestant school, and then in Cuba, still Protestants were different. So because you were Catholic, you had to win. Silly things, but in that moment, it was the way it was.

Well, to this final game all the Catholic schools came together—they were always enemies—but this day they were all Jesuits. On the other side were non-Catholics. So it became a game of religion. The game started and the other team started pointing: 2 points; 4 points; 6 points. And I called to the coach, "Call in Fidel. He will not lose. Call Fidel." And he sent in Fidel. Fidel came out took the ball, and from the very corner of the floor from the other side he threw the ball and put it in. And from that moment we started winning, and winning, and winning. He played fair, but different—his own style. You could only recommend him for that. He could not stand to lose.

So anyway, when we finished the game and we won by 25 points or something like that, everyone raced to Fidel and said, "Yea, yea Fidel you are the one, you are the one." And Fidel said to me, "Father, now I have to pray the rosaries to our lady for thirty days, because I promised if I won, I would pray for that." He was sixteen or seventeen years old.

He became one of the best in sports, but through sacrifices. For instance, these boys were boarders and were allowed to go to their families or friends on the weekends. Friday evening they would leave and come back on Sunday evening. But Fidel stayed always in the school practicing sports. This was very important for him.

The day of his graduation, for fifteen minutes they clapped, "Fidel, Fidel, Fidel!" when he passed to get his diploma. That's because he was the one for track—the 800 meters; 400 meters, he broke the records. And in basketball—very good, and of course, his studies were excellent. Oh yes, very brilliant. Always very good and without much effort. It came easy.

But he was quite disordered, quite unpredictable. For instance, he always had a problem inside that he came from the country. And being Fidel, though very brilliant, he always considered himself lower and that the people looked down at him. And that was terrible. Also, as you know, Fidel Castro is the son of a servant of his father's. He had him with a servant. It is important to know his problem. This was terrible. And really, in Spain and in Cuba, they were too tough with these cases. A bastard. So he hated society.

Although the father later married her, this was always a shadow over his life; he never could overcome it completely. Many times he said to me, "If I would not find you, I would say that I have no family."

His father was cold and tough, but was very proud of him because he knew he was the most intelligent of the children. He was rich, and Fidel Castro always had money in his pocket—"Look at the dollars." But he does not have anything for the money. Money means nothing to him. Nothing. Only power. Power.

Fidel is not Cuban, properly speaking; he's more a Spaniard in his character and personality. His specialty comes from a part of Spain where people are like steel. Galicia. His father was such a Spaniard.

There is a difference. For instance, Cubans are more friendly, not so stable, not so constant. A Cuban would already be tired of being in power. "That's okay, quite enough, quite enough." Not a Galician. No. Till death. For instance, Francisco Franco came from there. He died in power. Franco, Hitler, Mussolini, all who have power were his idols. He is a dictator by nature.

They say that Gallegos, those from that part of Spain, can be buried, but are not dead. You can imagine that, after the failure of Russia, and he still continues.

We had a group of explorers. Cuba is a very beautiful country, everywhere, and often on long weekends we would go to the mountains. One time I went with him and about forty other boys to the mountains. So immediately I have to name him the chief, because he was this.

That day we left our tent and crossed to the other side of the river, a river that came from the mountain. And just like that, it started raining enormously, like a flood. And were we going to reach the mountain? We did, but the whole day—raining, raining.

Later, when we came back it was still raining. I said, "Fidel, go and see how is the river. Is it going to be very easy to pass?" And he went to see and came back and said to me, "Father, the water is up to my chest." And I said, "Well anyhow, we have to go through, because we have here more than forty boys who are not as strong as you and me." They had their dry clothes on the other side of the river, their food, everything to sleep, so we had to go through. "What are we going to do? Fidel, you take this rope with your teeth because the water is going to take you and you must swim." So he said, "Okay, we'll do that." The water was twenty-five meters with strong currents, but he reached the other side. He tied the end of the rope to the tree and the boys went across. I remained to make sure the boys were safe. Last, I went, but I wanted to save the rope too. We needed a rope. And when I reached the river, the water took me up. Fidel was on the other side, but when he saw me go, he jumped in the river, and we embraced and cried and we came out. He said, "Father, it has been a miracle, and let us thank God for it." I say these things to let you know that in that moment Fidel Castro believed. How deep, I don't know.

Then one day two boys disappeared from the school. Well, no news about them. The radio, the newspaper, the parents were all preoccupied with trying to find them. Somehow, the director of the school knew that Fidel Castro knew about them. He called him in, "Fidel Castro, you know where these boys are?" "Yes." "Well, you have to tell." "No, I will not tell. I promised not to say anything." And the Father tried to convince him to tell, but he would not say a word.

Fidel Castro came to me and said, "Father, give me the key of the dormitory. I have to leave. The director expelled me from the school." "What happened to you?" And he told me. I knew the director well and hoped to work things out, so I said, "Fidel, you are not going to leave the school today. You will not go today, but in one week. In one week I will prepare for you your luggage and your things." I said, "Fidel, you always ask me many things and I always say yes, now I ask from you this." Well, he stayed the week.

What had happened? Three days before it was the Pearl Harbor and these boys wanted to fight against Japan with the Americans. Fidel Castro was going to do that too, but in the last moment he stayed. That's why he knew. So nothing happened.

Many times I had to intervene to solve problems with the teacher. Because Fidel would say to the teacher, "I don't agree." But what he said normally was right. That's why I backed him.

You can become a very good friend of his, but I found out later, he needed to be famous at any price. And this is the place where the abnormality appears—at any price. That's the problem. For instance, all are very good friends to him, but do not doubt him.

Fidel Castro is very difficult to define because he has many things different, different qualities. So in some way he's a bit Quixote—a dreamer, dreaming, always dreaming—and on another side a practical man in other things. So you cannot say that he was a model. A model is the common ordinary man who does well everything. No, Fidel Castro maybe does some things normal, but suddenly he does an extraordinary thing. So he is not the man of the ordinary things, but a man who does difficult things.

In his youth, boys would laugh, some would follow him, there was a mixture of different feelings, but nothing against him. He tried to persuade them, but if he did not convince them, he demanded they do it, and they followed. He was very cold, so to speak, with girls. He supposed that they could damage him—they could allow a weakness to appear. For him, he always had to be powerful, always himself. I never saw him dancing. And all the boys danced but him. No doubt that he was virile and quite a man, but not romantic.

We both left at the same time. I went back to Europe, and he went to the university. I knew that Fidel Castro was going to do something important. You see in the year-book when he was graduated, under his picture I wrote some saying like, "Fidel is a born hero. The history of his country will speak of him." That was in 1945; he was already a man, very mature. You could foresee his ideas. He wanted to become a name. And I told him many times, "You can become a great leader, the raw material is here. Do it for your country." I couldn't think like that for any other boy.

The best years of his life were in this school. Those three years were special. He was triumphant in every field.

Father Armando Llorente

PHOTOGRAPHS

Havana

PHOTOGRAPHS

Santiago de Cuba